# Grammar

C000183022

## Grammar

### Section 1 — Word Types

#### Page 2 — Nouns

1. Concrete nouns: **house**, **fish**, **grass**, **ball**, **bike**
   Abstract nouns: **faith**, **freedom**, **hope**, **anger**
   Collective nouns: **shoal**, **swarm**, **flock**, **herd**

2. Any suitable nouns. Examples:
   To get to the **butcher's**, I pass a field with a **flock** of **sheep**.
   The **excitement** I feel about going to **Birmingham** on the **train** is overwhelming.

#### Page 3 — Verbs

1. Drew **agrees** with his brother.
   We **are** going to **see** some friends tomorrow.
   He always **screams** when he sees a moth.
   Michael often **does** his homework straight after school.

2. **I am** captain of the county football team.
   I usually **dry my** wet hair with a towel.
   **I go** to night school twice a week.
   **I have** a new sports car.

#### Pages 4 and 5 — Modal Verbs

1. I **wouldn't** want to be famous.
   Tim **should** change his socks.
   Laura **may** know the answer.
   He **will** give us some advice.
   They **can** come too.
   Roger **should** know better.
   We **shall** do our very best.
   I **could** drive us there.
   Sally **might** move to Canada.
   You **ought** to know better.

2. Our holiday **should** have been relaxing, but it was very stressful.
   I **could** have gone with Johnny, but I had other things to do.
   That **might** be the answer, but I'm not so sure.
   Ken and Peter are away next week — they **must** let Katie know.
   The builders knew they **could** finish the job on time.
   I'm really not sure about what to do — I **might** ask a friend.
   Julie's not feeling well — she **ought** to stay in bed.

3. I **might** as well go to the party on my own.
   Norman would go on holiday to Australia if he **could** afford it.
   **Would** you like a piece of apple crumble?
   If you change your mind, you **should** let me know.
   300 ml of milk **ought** to be enough for the pancake mixture.

4. Any suitable.
   Examples:
   **I might go to watch a football match tomorrow.**
   **I must go to see the head teacher.**
   **I will eat all of this pudding.**
   **I should buy my brother a birthday present.**

#### Page 6 — Adjectives

1. You should have underlined: **aggressive**, **rare**, **dismal**, **odd**, **cheeky**, **purple**, **trendy**, **unusual**, **crazy**.

2. Any suitable adjectives.
   Examples:
   The play was **interesting** and the actors were **fabulous**.
   I had a **great** time.
   The concert was **awful** — the music was **terrible** and the food was **disgusting**.

3. Any suitable adjectives.
   Examples:
   There was a **strange** noise coming from the kitchen.
   The **enormous** monster in the cave is very angry.
   The **mischievous** monkeys will break our windscreen wipers.

#### Pages 7 to 9 — Adverbs

1. He played <u>well</u>. — **Verb**
   The party was <u>bitterly</u> disappointing. — **Adjective**
   The car is <u>incredibly</u> dirty. — **Adjective**
   Louise <u>cheerfully</u> waved to us. — **Verb**
   Sam seems <u>extremely</u> pleased. — **Adjective**

2. Tamina **accidentally** broke her mum's favourite vase.
   Olivia said she didn't feel **very** well.
   The ballerinas danced **elegantly** across the stage.
   The schoolboy **truthfully** answered the teacher's questions.
   That house is **severely** damaged.

3. Certain: **definitely**, **surely**, **certainly**
   Not certain: **maybe**, **perhaps**, **possibly**

4. Any suitable sentences with a less certain adverb.
   Examples:
   It's **possibly** true that the weather wasn't good enough.
   Setting a deadline will **maybe** make a difference.
   My car will **perhaps** break down on the way.

5. Any suitable sentences with a more certain adverb.
   Examples:
   We will **definitely** go to see Grandma tomorrow.
   Francis and Gillian are **certainly** going to the cinema tonight.
   **Surely** Ulvertown Rovers will win the league.

6. Any suitable sentences.
   Examples:
   **Perhaps the sun will come out this afternoon.**
   **Surely Jessica will be pleased with her results.**
   **Maybe the play will be a success.**
   **Karen is definitely the best player at our club.**

# *Grammar*

## *Page 10 — Pronouns*

1. Charlotte made a picture for Trudy, then gave **it** to **her**.
   Ed and Sam lost Mike, so **they** went to look for **him**.

2. I was cross with Dennis — **he** took my favourite CD
   and scratched **it**. He was sorry and said he would buy
   **me** a new one. My sister was angry with him too — he
   borrowed **her** scissors and broke **them** But never mind,
   **we** are all friends again now.

## *Page 11 — Relative Pronouns*

1. **We met the acrobat who performed in the circus.**
   **I like the blue shoes which have sparkly laces.**
   **They always stay in hotels which have a five-star rating.**
   **Paul is the builder who built our house.**
   **Lauren saw the dentist who gave her a filling.**

2. We have a new neighbour **who** works at the bank.
   This is the shop **which/that** sells diving equipment.
   That's the man **whose** son is a famous footballer.
   Geraldine owns a house **which/that** has four bedrooms
   and a big garden.

## *Page 12 — Determiners*

1. **The** teacher told us **a** funny story about **an** elephant in
   **the** jungle.
   We saw **a** picture of **that** house by **the** river where **your**
   boat is.
   Ben and Bill finally changed **those** light bulbs in **their**
   bathroom.
   **A** police officer chased **some** thieves out of **the** bank and
   into **an** alleyway.

2. Any suitable determiners.
   Examples:
   **That** pizza is the best pizza I've ever tasted.
   We need to go to the garage — **our** car has broken
   down.
   Add **some** milk — any amount is fine.
   Kelly saw **an** aardvark and **a** lion at the zoo.

## *Section 2 — Clauses and Phrases*

### *Page 13 — Clauses*

1. <u>Darius went to the shop</u> because he needed some milk.
   <u>Jodie is going to the party</u> even if Rebecca won't go with
   her.
   Provided that it doesn't start to rain, <u>they'll play outside</u>.
   Unless you know the answer, <u>we'll ask Richard</u>.
   <u>They climbed the tree</u> even though I thought it was a
   bad idea.

2. Any suitable clauses.
   Examples:
   We need to wait **until we're allowed to go in**.
   Eleanor has a shower **after going to the gym**.
   I'm going to buy some sweets **when we get to the shop**.
   Doris wants to get a dog **although her parents say
   she can't**.
   Sophie eats her breakfast **before going to school**.

## *Pages 14 and 15 — Basic Relative Clauses*

1. You should have circled the words in bold and
   underlined these clauses:
   I prefer the blue shoes **which** <u>match my dress</u>.
   This is the house **that** <u>Megan is going to move into</u>.
   I don't like people **who** <u>are cruel to animals</u>.
   We found a lost dog **whose** <u>owner was nowhere to be
   seen</u>.
   Yvonne likes to go for walks **that** <u>have amazing views</u>.
   This is the computer game **that** <u>I bought last weekend</u>.

2. This is the book **which/that** Pria was reading.
   The Tasty Taverna is a restaurant **which/that** specialises
   in vegetarian meals.
   I need to find a shop **which/that** sells fancy dress
   costumes.
   Ulrika met a man **whose** dog was almost as big as he
   was.
   Juliet is the person **who/that** always gets her own way.
   Let's go on holiday to a country **which/that** has hot,
   sunny weather.
   We saw a jellyfish **whose** tentacles were two metres
   long.

3. I found an injured rabbit whose leg was broken.
   Scott moved to a quiet village where there were no other
   children.
   Dad is looking for a builder who can renovate our house.
   Kevin remembers the day when he got lost at the funfair.
   Colin wants to buy the game that he saw advertised
   on TV.

4. Any suitable relative clauses.
   Examples:
   Susanna waited for Edward, **who was stuck in traffic**.
   There was a lot of noise, **which was very distracting**.
   Ronald went to the circus, **which had acrobats**.
   The people welcomed the man **who had a parrot on his
   shoulder**.

5. Any suitable sentences.
   Examples:
   The teacher, **who was very strict**, gave the class extra
   homework.
   The scientist made an everlasting cake, **which was his
   best experiment so far**.

## *Pages 16 and 17 — Trickier Relative Clauses*

1. After the party, **which finished at midnight**, we went to
   bed.
   The room **where the books are stored** is being repainted.
   Neil, **whose son plays the drums in a band**, loves rock
   music.
   That day **when I fell over** was the most embarrassing day
   of my life.
   The house **that flooded during the storm** can now be
   lived in again.
   Liam, **who wants to be a pilot**, is taking flying lessons.

2. Any suitable relative clauses.
   Examples:
   The boy **whose paper aeroplane had crashed** looked very angry.
   Michael's phone, **which cost a lot of money**, broke.
   The town **where Melissa is moving to** is not very big.
   Roger's nephew, **who plays the piano**, is twelve.
   That windy day **when our tent blew away** was awful.
   My old teddy bear, **which I've had for ten years**, is in the wash.

3. You should have ticked:
   The museum which we visited was very interesting.
   That's the football team that Josh is joining.
   My tenth birthday was the day that Feverton won the FA Cup.

4. The walk we went on was far too long.
   I've forgotten the name of the film Jim recommended.
   He can't remember the day we went to the zoo.

## Page 18 — Phrases

1. You should have circled: **this afternoon**, **on the way to school**, **a yellow submarine**, **really fast**.

2. Phrase: **behind the blue sofa**, **on the phone**, **little, pork sausages**, **at the back**, **those naughty boys**, **long, hairy legs**.
   Clause: **he's silly**, **Ray sat down**, **we're happy**, **let's play golf**, **I go swimming**, **they're fine**.

# Section 3 — Conjunctions and Prepositions

## Page 19 — Co-ordinating Conjunctions

1. I'd like to go to Australia, **but** it's too expensive.
   In the cellar it was dark, **and** there were lots of strange noises.
   Please give this letter to a parent, **or** give it to a guardian.
   Playing near busy roads is dangerous, **so** you shouldn't do it.
   Mabel felt completely relaxed, **for** she was on holiday.

2. I would like a drink **and** I would like some food.
   Fran's remark was hurtful, **but** it was also true.
   My teacher told me off, **so** I stopped talking.

## Page 20 — Subordinating Conjunctions

1. Help yourself to a glass of water <u>if</u> you are thirsty.
   <u>Unless</u> your dad says you can't, you can come to the cinema.
   <u>Although</u> it might sound silly, I quite like going for walks in the rain.
   Marian goes to see her uncle in hospital <u>when</u> she is not busy.
   Fletcher watches TV programmes <u>while</u> he eats his lunch.

2. I have lived here **since** I was five.
   I follow my brother **wherever** he goes.
   My sister always smiles **while** she is dancing.
   I like Pierre **even though** he can be a bit annoying.
   The dog can't come in **because** his paws are dirty.

## Page 21 — Using Conjunctions for Cohesion

1. Any suitable conjunctions used to join the sentences.
   Examples:
   I was going to miss the train, **so** I began to run.
   We might go shopping **or** we might go cycling.

2. Any suitable conjunctions used to make the passage flow better.
   Examples:
   School was closed today **because** the heating was broken. The pupils went home, **but** no one complained. They went to the park **while** the teachers stayed at school.

## Pages 22 and 23 — Prepositions

1. Any sentences using sensible prepositions.
   Examples:
   There are flowers **under the window**.
   There is a bird **on the roof**.
   There is a tree **next to the house**.
   There are bushes **around the house**.
   There is a path **in front of the house**.

2. You should have circled these words:
   That picture **on** the wall is absolutely horrible.
   I ate lots of popcorn **during** the film.
   Iris has been playing the guitar **since** 10 pm.
   Ronald is meeting his dad **in front of** the police station.
   We can't do anything **until** the day after tomorrow.
   Let's put up posters **in** any available space.
   They buried the time capsule **underneath** the oak tree.

3. **On** Friday, I'm going to the dentist.
   I think there's a mistake **in** my work.
   The man in the cinema told us to stop talking **during** the film.
   Our school is open **from** 8 am **until** 4 pm.
   The shop isn't open, so people are forming a queue **outside** the door.
   I always listen to music **after** dinner.

4. Any sentence that uses at least two prepositions correctly.
   Examples:
   I waited **outside** the cinema patiently **until** 9 pm.

5. Any sentences that use prepositions correctly.
   Examples:
   My bed is **in the middle of** the room. **Next to** the bed I have a small table, and **on** the table there is a lamp and a clock. My wardrobe is **at the end of** the room, **beside** the window. I have three posters **on** the walls.

# Grammar

## Section 4 — Linking Ideas

### Pages 24 and 25 — Linking Ideas in a Paragraph

1. You should have circled these phrases:
   over there
   after a while
   twice a year
   every time
   the other day
   near the wall
   very slowly

2. The chest was unlocked. <u>Without a sound</u>, Susie opened the lid.
   It's a hot day. You should put suncream on <u>after lunch</u>.
   I do after-school activities <u>four times a week</u>. It's exhausting but fun.
   There are one hundred tadpoles <u>in the school pond</u>. We're studying them.
   The bus arrived. Thomas ate his breakfast <u>ridiculously fast</u>.
   There was so much to do. Tina didn't stop painting <u>until midnight</u>.
   My bedroom was a mess. I hid all the toys and books <u>under the bed</u>.

3. Yesterday, I went to an amazing activity day. <u>First</u> we had to register, and then we played some warm-up games. <u>At 10 am</u>, we raced each other through a great obstacle course. We ate <u>in the garden</u>, and <u>after lunch</u> we built a big tree house. <u>Finally</u> we made rafts and raced them <u>in two separate teams</u>.

4. Example sentences:
   I am making a kite. After tea, I will try it out.
   The witch looked around. She crept up the stairs very quietly.
   It is Christmas Eve. Tomorrow morning, it will be Christmas Day.

### Pages 26 and 27 — Linking Paragraphs

1. You should have matched these pairs:
   <u>Later</u>, the nurse looked at my ankle. She said it was broken in two places. — time
   <u>Thirdly</u>, I started to screw the different pieces together, one at a time. — number
   <u>At Grandad's house</u>, Clare set up the chessboard and made two cups of tea. — place

2. You should have drawn lines to match these words and phrases:
   Place: in Ian's room, next to him, at the garage, above that, behind me
   Number: secondly, thirdly, fourthly, firstly
   Time: this week, at 5 pm, before breakfast, every day

3. In the morning, George went to buy the ingredients for his lemon cake. It took over an hour.
   <u>That afternoon</u>, he started mixing and measuring.

   Secondly, I covered the exercise book in colourful patterned paper.
   <u>Thirdly</u>, I used some sticky plastic to make the book waterproof and keep it looking neat.

   My brother Jeremy loves doing science experiments — even in the house!
   <u>Last week</u>, he mixed lots of Mum's hair products together. It exploded everywhere!

   I was really enjoying the spaghetti Dad had made for tea, but I kept dropping bits accidentally.
   <u>Under the table</u>, our cat was eating the scraps, but he couldn't manage the spaghetti!

4. Any two sentences where the first sentence begins with an adverbial phrase which has been used correctly. Examples:
   <u>All of a sudden</u>, PC Collins spotted something shiny under a crate. It had to be the stolen jewels!
   <u>Earlier that day</u>, I had seen my sister make a huge chocolate tart. I knew it would be in there, waiting for me to try it.

## Section 5 — Verb Tenses

### Page 28 — Present Tense and Past Tense

1. <u>pack</u> — We packed the car.
   <u>pay</u> — I paid the bills.
   <u>throw</u> — They threw it out.
   <u>paints</u> — He painted a picture.
   <u>does</u> — Hannah did a lot.

2. Any sentences about the pictures which are in the correct tense.
   Examples:
   Present: The villain sneaks around.
   Past: The robber crept away from the police.
   Present: The man holds the spanner.
   Past: The mechanic fixed the car.

### Page 29 — Verbs with 'ing'

1. We were starting, but they were finishing.
   Mark and Katie were skiing, but I was freezing!
   I was running, he was jogging and they were sitting.

2. My brother Micah is **leaving** home today. Six months ago he was **applying** to boarding school, and he was **hoping** to get a place. Now he is actually **going**. I will miss him because he is always **helping** me with my homework. I am already **counting** down the days until half term.

*Targeted Answer Book for Year 5 — Grammar*  © CGP 2014

## *Page 30 — Past Tense with 'have'*

1. Tamara has decided not to move house.
   Martha has been to the shops.
   Ralph has taken Lilly's chocolate.

2. I have planned a surprise for Ann because she has passed her exams. I have chosen a really good film at the cinema, and I have booked tickets for us.

## Section 6 — Standard and non-Standard English

### *Pages 31 and 32 — Standard and Non-Standard English*

1. He were an amazing player. — N
   I am going fishing today. — S
   Last week, I run five miles. — N
   Have you finished your dinner? — S
   You are very tall, Mr Grew. — S
   I will played sport later. — N
   That are an awful story. — N
   We are listening to music. — S
   I eat two muffins yesterday. — N
   I am building a spaceship. — S

2. You should have crossed out these words:
   I (saw / ~~seen~~) my grandparents earlier when they (came / ~~come~~) over.
   You should (have / ~~of~~) asked before you (~~done~~ / did) it without me.
   I would (have / ~~of~~) asked Stuart, but he (~~gone~~ / went) home.
   Jerry (~~come~~ / came) downstairs because he had (done / ~~did~~) his homework.
   We might (have / ~~of~~) left the pencils where we (~~done~~ / did) the drawing.
   Kevin must (have / ~~of~~) (gone / ~~went~~) on another special mission.

3. those
   them
   those
   I
   me
   me

4. Any suitable sentences that use the correct grammar.
   Examples:
   I am not very well.
   We are not sure.
   Raj is not going.
   Becky has not got it.

5. I haven't got nothing. — 2
   My dad hasn't got a beard. — 1
   We don't have no biscuits left. — 2
   Michael won't go nowhere. — 2
   I can't tell you the secret. — 1
   They haven't got a sister. — 1
   You can't see nothing in here. — 2
   David doesn't like broccoli. — 1
   No one said nothing to me. — 2
   We mustn't do anything yet. — 1
   Oliver couldn't find anyone. — 1
   Clara wasn't helping no one. — 2

# *Punctuation*

## *Punctuation*

### *Section 1 — Sentence Punctuation*

#### *Page 2 — Capital Letters and Full Stops*

1. You should have circled: eiffel tower, spain, ashley, friday, christmas

2. You should have ticked:
   My dad's favourite sweets can only be bought in Canada.
   Jack's dog is called Spot.  Spot is a Dalmatian.
   I play cricket every Friday evening.
   Corrected sentences:
   **M**rs Flint is thirty-two**.  H**er birthday is in **M**ay.
   My **b**est **f**riend is called Amy.  She lives in Bath**.**

#### *Page 3 — Question Marks*

1. Where are you going on holiday**?**
   Here are those gloves you lost.
   Let's go shopping tomorrow.
   Is this your idea of a joke**?**
   Would you like ketchup**?**
   Are you feeling OK, Kelly**?**
   I don't know how to fry an egg.
   What's happening out there**?**
   It's raining a lot this week**.**
   We should order pizzas**.**

2. Any sensible question that begins with a capital letter and ends with a question mark.
   Examples:
   **W**ho would like to take the map**?**
   **W**hat shall I bring with me**?**
   **W**ould you like some chicken**?**
   **C**an you pick me up from Annie's later**?**

#### *Page 4 — Exclamation Marks*

1. You should have ticked:
   Shut up
   Stop that, now
   Quick, get out of here

2. Ouch, that really hurt**!**
   My brother is really good at playing the piano**.**
   Watch out, it's going to fall over**!**
   The bathroom is the second door on the left**.**

3. Any sentences that show strong emotion or something that would be said loudly and end with an exclamation mark.
   Examples:
   Thanks for inviting me to this wonderful party**!**
   I've had an absolutely terrible day**!**

#### *Page 5 — Sentence Practice*

1. Jon asked when they were leaving.  **(statement)**
   How ridiculous those shoes are!  **(exclamation)**
   Switch the appliance off at the mains.  **(command)**
   What time do you think we should leave?  **(question)**
   What an incredible cake that is!  **(exclamation)**

2. Any suitable sentences that use capital letters and punctuation correctly.
   Example:
   **H**arry is on holiday, and he wants to go sightseeing**.**
   **A**re you ready to be chopped up, little vegetables**?**
   **O**h no — my racket is broken and I don't have a spare one**!**

### *Section 2 — Commas*

#### *Pages 6 and 7 — Commas in Lists*

1. I am going to the supermarket with my mum, her sister and my best friend.  We need to buy some more cereal, a couple of pints of milk, a pack of dishcloths and some baking ingredients.  We are going to bake some chocolate-chip cookies, a batch of flapjacks, a sponge cake and a raspberry cheesecake.  We haven't got any flour, butter, sugar or raspberries at the moment.

2. You will need 500 g sugar, 200 g flour, 300 g butter and some raisins.
   Please bring a packed lunch, a swimming costume and a few pens.
   The journey was quite long, very tiring and really boring.

3. I need to clean the kitchen, bake some flapjacks, do my homework and tidy my bedroom.

4. Enter the competition to win a microwave, a brand-new camera, a week's supply of cake **or** (OR **and**) two theatre tickets.
   On the walk we saw a herd of cows, lots of benches, a squirrel **and** two rabbits.

#### *Pages 8 and 9 — Commas to Join Sentences*

1. You should have ticked:
   She is a brilliant mathematician, and she is good at science.
   Corrected sentences:
   I haven't been selected, nor do I expect to be.
   People try to beat us, yet they never succeed.

2. I will play tiddlywinks, but I want to finish this first.
   They didn't have what I wanted, so I bought this instead.
   We should hide the evidence, or we will be in trouble.

3. I tried to fly my kite, **but** there wasn't enough wind.
   It rained all day, **so** we stayed inside.
   I really like dancing, **and** I am quite good at it.
   We could get him a games console, **or** we could buy him a new jacket.

4. We played rounders, **but** (or **and**) the other team won.
   I like sausages and ice cream, **but** I do not like them on the same plate.
   I had a big breakfast, **so** I'm not really hungry now.

5. Any sensible sentence that uses a comma and a conjunction to join two main clauses.
   Example:
   The fireman rushed to put out the fire, **and** he saved the house from burning down.

# Punctuation

## Pages 10 and 11 — Commas After Subordinate Clauses

1. Once I'd finished eating, I started reading my new book.
As I got on the bus, I dropped my bag.
Although I am scared of sharks, I love visiting the aquarium.
Rather than going out, we stayed in and watched a film.

2. <u>While you were distracted</u>, I swapped our plates.
You can go to the party <u>as long as you wear something sensible</u>.
<u>Now that you've told me that</u>, everything makes much more sense.
<u>Until we've found the solution</u>, we'll keep trying to work it out.
I'll come and help you <u>as soon as I can</u>.
<u>Since we're all here</u>, I'd like to tell you something.

3. The sentences that need commas are:
When I realised what I'd done, I apologised immediately.
Although I like the album, this song isn't my favourite.
As you're older than me, you should go first.

4. Even though it was cold, I wanted ice cream.
Despite the fact we lost, we still had fun.
Whereas Tom is calm, Tim is always stressed.
Before I left the house, I turned the lights off.

5. Any correct subordinate clause that ends with a comma.
Examples:
After I've eaten, I need to ring my sister.
Despite Ollie's rude comments, Jim wasn't offended.
Even though the film was very frightening, Simon wasn't scared.

## Pages 12 and 13 — Commas After Introductions

1. As quietly as possible, James crept downstairs.
Very quickly, Emily jumped out of bed.
In ten years' time, my parents will be sixty.
Earlier today, my teacher gave me detention.
In a very silly way, Jack skipped across the yard.
In the kitchen, there's a present for you.

2. You should have ticked:
Before dawn, everything is very peaceful.
As quickly as possible, he packed his bags.
Under the new rules, we can't wear jewellery to school.
Corrected sentences:
In Italy, pizza and pasta are very popular foods.
Last week, the boys won the football match.

3. Before school, Kim made her packed lunch.
On Tuesday, I am going to the cinema.
Every morning, my dad runs 5 km.
In town, there is a really big skate park.

4. On the left, you can see my old house.
Every year, we visit my aunt.
Like a mouse, he crept through the house.
Earlier than usual, she set off for school.

## Pages 14 and 15 — Commas for Extra Information

1. You should have ticked:
The flight, even though it felt really long, only took three hours.
Dr Grey, our family doctor, told me to try to get more sleep.
Corrected sentences:
My brothers, who are twins, are called Jim and Joe.
We saw my teacher, Mr Harris, in the park.

2. On Thursday, the day after tomorrow, I am going on holiday. I am going with my two sisters, Becky and Charlotte, and our mum. We're spending a few days in Portugal, a really hot country, before flying back to England. The holiday, which was quite expensive, should be really fun.

3. The charity auction, which raised hundreds of pounds, was a great success.
Pepperoni, my favourite pizza topping, is a kind of sausage.
The shepherd, who'd lost all his sheep, was very upset.

4. Charles Dickens, a famous English writer, was born in 1812.
My pet mice, called Sammy and Sally, are adorable.
My parents, who met fifteen years ago, get on really well.

## Pages 16 and 17 — Comma Practice

1. You should have ticked:
The Alps, a European mountain range, are popular with skiers.
At the beach, I had an ice cream and read my book.
My favourite fruits are apples, oranges, pears and strawberries.
I didn't have any money, so I couldn't buy any sweets.
Corrected sentences:
The bus stops on King Street, Russel Lane and Victoria Square.
The book, about electricity, looks quite difficult.
We tried to get tickets, but they had sold out.
Even if I knew it, I wouldn't tell you the answer.

2. Many people came to the fair <u>until it started to rain</u>.
<u>While she was shopping</u>, we prepared her surprise.
<u>Even though I love most fruits</u>, I hate apples.
<u>If I get home in time</u>, I'll start making our tea.
<u>Although the pirate was very scary</u>, his parrot was hilarious.
You can help me with the decorations <u>since you're so early</u>.
<u>Provided that you've brought your trunks</u>, we can go swimming today.
You can't go to football practice <u>unless you've done your homework</u>.

3. We played hockey , **and** we won.
She can dance, **but** she can't sing.
You can eat now, **or** you can eat later.
He couldn't see, **so** he put his glasses on.

# Punctuation

## Section 3 — Brackets and Dashes

### Pages 18 and 19 — Brackets for Extra Information

1. You should have ticked:
   Rhinos (an endangered species) mostly live in Africa.
   Daniel was late to work yesterday (Tuesday).
   The competition was won by Mr Fairclough (a train driver).
   Our neighbour (Mrs Bewley) forgot to put the bins out.

2. Our friends (James and David) live across the road.
   It was too hot (thirty-six degrees) for the cat to go outside.
   (When we went fishing (last weekend), I caught nothing.
   The majority of the crowd (seventy-five) per cent) wanted Gareth to win.
   Jayne and Steve (our aunt and uncle) gave us a new sofa.

3. The portrait (painted in 1839) cost Mr Dough a lot of money.
   Fatima finished her knitting (a woolly jumper).
   There are eleven players (including a goalkeeper) in a hockey team.
   Rob's tie (black with sparkly bits) had a hole in it.

4. Jane and Barbara (the identical twins) work at the same shop.
   Arthur Coddle (an English author) wrote several novels.
   The café is closed on Mondays (the manager's day off).
   The poodle (a breed of dog) has lots of fur.
   'The Rising Sea' (my favourite book) is about mermaids.

5. Any suitable phrases.
   Examples:
   The main course (roast beef) was delicious.
   Hazel's dog (a Cocker Spaniel) likes to chase tennis balls.
   The workers (who were on strike) didn't turn up for work.
   Jenny's favourite toy (a rag doll) was very old.
   Rodney's car (a yellow three-wheeler) pulled up outside.
   The supermarket (the one at the end of the street) is overrun by mice.

### Pages 20 and 21 — Dashes for Extra Information

1. You should have crossed this sentence:
   We built — a sandcastle a big one — on the beach.
   The correct sentence is:
   We built a sandcastle — a big one — on the beach.

2. Mr Miller — the county's finest baker — has announced his plans to bake Britain's first gingerbread hotel. The hotel — four storeys high — will open next summer. Six thousand people — many from the local area — have applied to stay at the hotel during the first month. Mr Miller's son — also a baker — will be in charge of the construction of the hotel. Two tonnes of ginger — grown specially by Mr Miller — will be used in the project. Tim Bury — a famous architect — thinks that the plan will simply not work.

3. Moussa and Sonny — the carpenters — need some new tools.
   There is a box of chocolates — a big box — in the kitchen.
   Adam forgot his lunch — yet again — this morning.
   Hayley — a famous comedian — is performing tonight.

4. My cat — a tabby — likes to eat tuna.
   Lea's mum — a talented singer — is in the opera.
   The waltzer — a type of ride — makes me dizzy.

## Section 4 — Apostrophes

### Page 22 — Apostrophes for Missing Letters

1. she will — she'll
   they have — they've
   who would — who'd
   he is — he's
   they are — they're
   where is — where's
   that will — that'll
   must not — mustn't

2. Any sentences which use shortened versions of the words correctly.
   Examples:
   We should've gone the other way.
   He might've been quicker than you think.
   That won't work very well.
   They could've gone to the park.

### Page 23 — Apostrophes for Single Possession

1. puppy's
   bus's
   Jess's
   kite's
   pot's

2. You should have added an apostrophe and an 's' to these words:
   Ellenby's
   Rosie's
   Ahmed's
   band's
   Robin's

3. Any two sentences which use an apostrophe and an 's' to show possession correctly.
   Examples:
   The man's tie is spotty.
   The cowboy's trousers are red.

# Punctuation

## Page 24 — Apostrophes for Plural Possession

1. You should have crossed out these phrases:
   the sisters's
   the womens'
   the birds's
   the mices'

2. the students' books are heavy
   the dice's spots are black
   the guitars' strings are metal
   the children's bricks are blue
   the owls' eyes are big

## Page 25 — Its and It's

1. You should have ticked:
   It's fun to travel abroad.
   It's taken no time at all.
   It's my birthday today.
   The lion chased its prey.
   The baby threw its toys.
   Corrected sentences:
   It's got to work this time.
   The panda ate its dinner.
   It's time to go home now.

2. **It's** not dark outside yet.
   **Its** stripes are black and white.
   **Its** park has a jungle gym.
   **It's** important to eat fruit.
   **Its** sign is falling down.
   **It's** the busiest shop in town.
   **Its** home is under the floor.
   **It's** got to be finished later.

## Pages 26 and 27 — Apostrophe Practice

1. what will — what'll
   are not — aren't
   you would — you'd
   who is — who's
   when is — when's
   does not — doesn't

2. 

| is not | isn't | | let us | let's |
|---|---|---|---|---|
| where will | where'll | | has not | hasn't |
| why is | why's | | we would | we'd |
| have not | haven't | | he is (OR) he has | he's |
| might have | might've | | should not | shouldn't |

3. You should have added these apostrophes:
   My **hamster's** name is Hector, and **I've** had him for two years.
   The shark showed its teeth and swam towards the **fisherman's** boat.
   **It's** been a great day, but now the park is shutting its gates.
   **Dina's** going to her **dad's** house tomorrow because **it's** Wednesday.

4. The cars' old engines
   The women's red coats
   The dresses' thin straps
   The tigers' sharp claws
   The men's good work

5. You should have matched these pairs:
   the girl's cats — one girl owns two cats
   the girls' cats — two girls own two cats
   the girl's cat — one girl owns one cat
   the girls' cat — two girls own one cat

6. Any two sentences where one uses 'its' correctly and the other uses 'it's' correctly.
   Examples:
   The rabbit is eating its carrot.
   It's a rabbit eating a carrot.

## Section 5 — Inverted Commas

## Pages 28 and 29 — Punctuating Speech

1. Fred said happily, "This is going to be the best weekend ever."
   "Rachel, stop that at once!" shouted her aunt.
   "Please may I buy some sweets to take home?" asked Hannah.
   Charlotte said, "We need to take a packed lunch with us today."
   "I want to go and see the tigers first," said Anna excitedly.

2. "Are you going to the party"? asked Tom. — punctuation mark in the wrong place
   Dad shouted, "dinner is ready!" — missing capital letter
   Emily said "I have a baby brother." — missing comma
   "I'm practising all the time", said Max. — punctuation mark in the wrong place
   "This cookie is delicious " said Sophie. — missing comma
   My sister asked, "is this your skirt?" — missing capital letter
   Nasreen shouted "Come here please!" — missing comma

3. The children shouted, "We love Grantham School Hockey Team!"
   "Today I am going to talk about my hobby," said Nicholas.
   "What are we going to do with this monkey?" asked Molly.
   "Have you got your passport and your ticket?" my aunt asked.
   Yasmin yelled, "I can see the theme park over there!"
   "Can we change the channel, please?" asked Yusif.

4. "I don't feel very well at all," said Ben.
   Jasmine asked, "How do I get to the station?"
   "There's a fire in the gym!" yelled William.

5. Any sentence which uses inverted commas correctly with the words in the box.
   Example:
   "Did you score at football today?" Mum asked.

# Punctuation

## *Page 30 — Punctuating Speech in Two Parts*

1. You should have ticked these sentences:
   "At long last," said the villain, "the whole world will be mine!"
   "Excuse me," said the lady, "do you know what time it starts?"

2. "This drink," said Guy, "tastes of nothing."
   "I think," said Rob, "it's just round here."
   "And then," said Sam, "he just disappeared!"

3. "I think," said Gwen, "that we should all go."
   "Just focus," said Dan, "and it will be fine."

## *Section 6 — Paragraphs and Layout*

### *Page 31 — Paragraphs*

1. You should have added these paragraph markers:
   "This is hopeless," moaned Jane, "I can't do it." The maths exercise had taken her most of the lesson already. // "It's easy," said Jack. "You're forgetting to add the seven, that's all." // Jane wasn't impressed. She covered the page with her arms and scowled at him. // "Don't worry, Jack" said Tracy. "Jane never lets anyone help."
   You should have rewritten the passage like this:
   "This is hopeless," moaned Jane, "I can't do it." The maths exercise had taken her most of the lesson already.
   "It's easy," said Jack. "You're forgetting to add the seven, that's all."
   Jane wasn't impressed. She covered the page with her arms and scowled at him.
   "Don't worry, Jack," said Tracy. "Jane never lets anyone help."

### *Page 32 — Headings and Subheadings*

1. You should have matched these pairs:
   Welcome to Paradise — An advert for a luxury holiday
   A Treat for Your Taste Buds — A review of a local restaurant
   More Than Just Books — A leaflet promoting the library

2. Any three subheadings which match the content of the paragraphs.
   Examples:
   The Best Quality Teaching
   After-School Activities for All
   Top of the Range Technology

# *Spelling*

## *Spelling*

### *Section 1 — Prefixes*

#### *Pages 2 and 3 — Prefixes — 'under' 'over' 'en' and 'em'*

1. **over**slept, **over**grown, **under**staffed, **under**populated, **over**crowded, **under**qualified

2. **paid** — overpaid, underpaid
**value** — overvalue, undervalue

3. **em**bolden, **en**courage, **en**act, **en**rage, **em**pathise, **em**power, **en**danger, **en**circle, **en**force

4. **enlarge, enliven, embitter, enclose**

5. Any sentence where the word is used correctly.
Examples:
Frank bought an **oversized** T-shirt.
I think the new Shakespeare film is **underrated**.
The kite string got **entangled** in the trees.

#### *Pages 4 and 5 — Prefixes — 'mid' 'pre' 'fore' and 'non'*

1. The **mid**term test will take place on Tuesday.
If you would like to take part, you need to **pre**register.
The problem with pollution is at the **fore**front of the agenda.

2. **pre**mature, **fore**head, **non**fiction, **fore**ground, **pre**date, **mid**way, **mid**summer, **mid**week, **pre**program

3. **fore**see, **pre**book, **mid**morning, **non**refillable, **mid**air, **fore**court

4. **forecast, midfielder, midsection, preschool, midday, Midwinter, preselected, preview**

5. The jungle ball ends at **midnight** with fireworks.
I can't understand my little brother —
he speaks **nonsense**.
Crocodiles look like **prehistoric** creatures.
The workers received instructions from the **foreman**.
The children were at the **midpoint** of the project.

#### *Pages 6 and 7 — Hyphenating Prefixes*

1. **re-examine, pro-American, co-ordinate, re-emerge, pre-order, co-exist**

2. **pre-own, re-elect, anti-American, re-enter, anti-ageing, pro-European, co-owner**

3. Penelope **re-sent** her letter to the major after receiving no reply.
Brad didn't **resent** the fact that Stu beat him in the 100 m hurdles.
We need to **re-cover** our sofa — it's very tatty.
Ashley has still not **recovered** from the operation.
Many people are against the government's plans for **reform**.
The synchronised swimmers **re-formed** to create a heart shape.
Henry used invisible ink by mistake, so he had to **re-sign** the form.
Julie had an argument with her boss and decided to **resign**.

After mixing up the documents, we had to **re-sort** them.
We had to **resort** to pushing our car to the garage.

4. I help my friends as much as possible — it's good to **co**-operate.
Ann and Jim are **co**-authors of a best-selling novel.
No one applied for the job, so the position will be **re**-advertised.

5. Any sentence where the word has been used correctly.
Examples:
Thank you very much for your **co-operation**.
The government has developed a new range of **anti-aircraft** missiles.

### *Section 2 — Word Endings and Suffixes*

#### *Pages 8 and 9 — Word Endings — the 'shun' sound*

1. You should have underlined: **mencian, hesitacian, attencian, beautition**.
The correct spellings are: **mention, hesitation, attention, beautician**.

2. **musician, invitation, friction, mathematician, optician, completion**

3. colli**sion**, permi**ssion**, deci**sion**, ten**sion**, conclu**sion**, intru**sion**

4. in**tention**, ma**gician**, dis**cussion**, op**eration**, el**ectrician**, so**lution**

#### *Page 10 — Word Endings — the 'shus' sound*

1. overcau**tious**, suspi**cious**, cons**cious**, atro**cious**

2. **fictitious, vicious, delicious, precious**

3. Any sentence where the word is used correctly.
Examples:
**Infectious** diseases can sometimes spread quickly.
Julian is very **ambitious**.
I try to eat a **nutritious** meal every day.

#### *Page 11 — Word Endings — the 'shul' sound*

1. **potential, special, confidential, initial**

2. mar**tial**, essen**tial**, artifi**cial**, so**cial**, substan**tial**, influen**tial**

3. **racial, partial, spacial**

#### *Pages 12 and 13 — Word Endings — 'ant' and 'ent'*

1. You should have ticked: **independent** and **innocent**.
You should have crossed: **arrogent, instrumant, hesitent** and **expectent**.
The correct spellings are: **arrogant, instrument, hesistant** and **expectant**.

2. dec**ent**, relev**ant**, toler**ant**, perman**ent**, evid**ent**, dist**ant**, tal**ent**

# Spelling

3. You should have circled: **commant**, **vacent**, **independant**, **anciant**.
   The correct spellings are: **comment**, **vacant**, **independent**, **ancient**.

4. Across: 1. **elephant** 2. **comment**
   Down: 1. **accident** 2. **silent** 3. **absent** 4. **present**

## Pages 14 and 15 — Word Endings — 'ance', 'ancy' and 'ence', 'ency'

1. **science**, **reference**, **patience**, **guidance**, **balance**

2. **decency**, **resistance**, **evidence**, **influence**, **efficiency**, **urgency**, **reliance**

3. independ**ence**, intellig**ence**, subst**ance**, experi**ence**

4. **vacancy**, **emergency**, **frequency**, **pregnancy**, **expectancy**

5. **performance**, **currency**, **fragrance**, **absorbency**, **guidance**

## Pages 16 and 17 — Word Endings — 'able', 'ible', 'ably' and 'ibly'

1. **reasonably**, **adjustable**, **flexible**, **incredibly**

2. considerable — **considerably**
   applicable — **applicably**
   horrible — **horribly**
   responsible — **responsibly**
   reliable — **reliably**
   comfortable — **comfortably**
   adorable — **adorably**

3. accept**able**, change**able**, ined**ible**, sens**ibly**, question**able**, terr**ibly**, understand**ably**, miser**ably**

4. Any sentence where the word is used correctly.
   Examples:
   Heather found her dinner really **enjoyable**.
   Rachael did **remarkably** well in the bike race.
   The mountains became **visible** when the Sun came up.
   Anthony wrote more **legibly** after practising.
   The school was **accessible** for Ed's wheelchair.

## Pages 18 and 19 — Suffixes

1. fam**ous**, angr**ily**, humor**ous**, scar**ily**

2. You should have ticked: **simplify** and **criticise**.
   You should have crossed: **justiceify**, **activeate**, **memoryise**, **terrorify**.
   The correct spellings are: **justify**, **activate**, **memorise**, **terrify**.

3. **advertise**, **decorate**, **summarise**, **classify**, **hyphenate**

4. author**ise**, origin**ate**, not**ify**, special**ise**, capital**ise**

5. Any sentence where the word is used correctly.
   Examples:
   Dylan was able to sympath**ise** with Viv's situation.
   Seeing a skeleton is enough to horr**ify** anyone.
   I am still waiting for Gareth to apolog**ise**.

# Section 3 — Confusing Words

## Pages 20 and 21 — ei and ie Words

1. shr**ie**k, sh**ie**ld, f**ie**ld, w**ei**ght

2. c**ei**ling, pr**ie**st, rec**ei**ve, rel**ie**ve, gr**ie**f, bel**ie**ve, conc**ei**ve, dec**ei**ve.

3. You should have made: **piece**, **thief**, **chief**

4. **relieved**, **neighbour**, **friend**, **seize**

5. The answers to the clues are: **caffeine**, **receipt**, **thief**, **niece**, **brief**

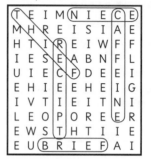

## Pages 22 and 23 — Words with 'ough' in

1. Words with 'ow' sound: **plough**, **bough**
   Words with 'or' sound: **fought**, **thought**, **sought**, **nought**
   Words with 'off' sound: **trough**, **cough**

2. **tough**, **enough**, **rough**

3. You should have linked: **bough** and **plough**, **borough** and **thorough**, **though** and **dough**, **brought** and **ought**.

4. **thoughtful**, **although**, **trough**, **nought**

5. **enough**, **ought**, **Throughout**, **bought**, **thorough**, **tough**

6. Any sentence where the word is used correctly.
   Examples:
   We went **through** the tunnel rather than over the mountain.
   Patrick was very **thorough** when checking for mistakes.
   I'm going to football practice even **though** I feel a bit ill.

## Pages 24 and 25 — Words with Silent Letters

1. ex**h**aust, w**h**en, **g**uess, **k**now, lis**t**en, **h**our, **k**nee, com**b**

2. i**s**land, lam**b**, this**t**le, si**g**n, cal**f**, **g**host

3. Silent w words: **s**word, ans**w**er, **w**rite
   Silent h words: **w**hirl, **w**heat, **w**histle
   Silent g words: campai**g**n, **g**nome
   Silent b words: lim**b**, plum**b**er

4. **knocked**, **climbed**, **school**, **sign**, **knife**, **honest**, **scent**

5. **Wednesday**, **often**, **debt**, **Autumn**, **guess**

6. Any sentence where the word is used correctly.
   Examples:
   I was so hungry I ate everything — I didn't leave a **crumb**.
   It's time to **knuckle** down to some homework.
   Morris writes a **column** for a local newspaper.

# Spelling

## Pages 26 and 27 — Unstressed Vowels

1. different, temperature, interesting, envelope, easily, personal, information, economical, fattening, frightening, offering, original

2. general, jewellery, describe, boundary, poison, family, library

3. refrigerate, confident, vegetable, memory, doctor, concentrate, business, marvellous

4. Unstressed e: miserable, intelligence, desperate, deafening,
   Unstressed a: miniature, parliament, secretary, valuable

5. **dictionary, voluntary, literature, separate**

6. Any sentence where the word is used correctly.
   Examples:
   Jack was a very **generous** individual.
   Maya's **favourite** toy is a little giraffe.
   A badger is an **animal** that lives in the UK.

## Pages 28 and 29 — Homophones

1. dessert, heel, mail

2. **guest, guessed, father, farther, herd, heard**

3. night — **knight**, bawl — **ball**, beech — **beach**, daze — **days**, blue — **blew**, pane — **pain**, steel — **steal**

4. coarse (**course**), led (**lead**), lone (**loan**), leak (**leek**), worn (**warn**)

Any sentence where the word is used correctly.
   Examples:
   The train remained **stationary** for five minutes.
   I think you'll find a stapler in the **stationery** cupboard.
   The first point should **precede** the second.
   Let's **proceed** with the meeting.

## Section 4 — Mixed Practice

### Pages 30 to 32 — Mixed Practice

1. achieve, receipt, retrieve, hygiene, mischief, cashier, perceive, shriek

2. You should have ticked: **independent, emergency, intelligence, impossible**
   You should have crossed: **referance, relevent, currancy, horrable, miserible**
   The correct spellings are: **reference, relevant, currency, horrible, miserable**

3. Words with 'shul' ending: **influential, special, partial, artificial**
   Words with 'shun' ending: **technician, television, operation, fiction**
   Words with 'shus' ending: **gracious, ambitious, spacious, anxious**

4. You should have circled: recieved, dougt, mourning, relevent, key
   The correct spellings are: received, doubt, morning, relevant, quay

5. Words with 'uff' sound: **tough, rough, enough**
   Words with 'oh' sound: **although, though, dough**
   Words with 'or' sound: **sought, thought, nought**

6. outrageous, gracefully, simplify, indicate, specialise

7. You should have made the words: **underwear, preview, enlarge, overload, midday, embolden, forename, nonsense**
   The hidden message is: **well done**

8. Any sentence where the words are used correctly.
   Examples:
   I decided I was going to **build** my new house myself.
   I'm sure the **rain** is more intense in the Lake District than elsewhere. OR I had to **rein** in my horse.
   I wore the **peak** of my cap down to hide my face.

*Targeted Answer Book for Year 5 — Spelling*

For indoor or outdoor use only

ISBN 978 1 78294 152 1

9 781782 941521

E5SA21

£2.00
(Retail Price)

www.cgpbooks.co.uk